MW01289167

Leadership Principles

Everything You Need to Know to Inspire, Motivate, and Lead!

We hope you enjoy this book
from The fREADom Library.

Peter Oliver

LEADERSHIP PRINCIPLES

Copyright © 2017 by Concise Reads™

DISCLAIMER: The author's books are only meant to provide the reader with the basic knowledge of a certain topic, without any warranties regarding whether the reader will, or will not, be able to incorporate and apply all the information provided. Although the author and publisher have made every effort to ensure that the information in this book

CONCISE READS™

Concise Reads was created to distill complex material into small morsels of knowledge that can be readily consumed by today's busy reader. At its core, Concise Reads is a living breathing brand that focuses on feeding knowledge to our always hungry entrepreneurial spirits. This knowledge is what we want to learn but without paying thousands of dollars for formal courses.

How much knowledge and how little time you spend to understand it, *together*, define value. We hope you enjoy the concise bits of value in the Concise Reads books, and we hope to continue to create more titles with time.

INTRODUCTION

"Leadership cannot be taught. It can only be learned."
Harold S. Geneen

"Tell me, and I will forget. Show me, and I may remember. Involve me, and I will understand."
Confucius, circa 450 BC

Leadership is not a buzzword. Leaders are not born. Ask Jack Welsh. They are made. Leaders are not all tall or beautiful. Tall and beautiful helps with persuasion, and that is only one principle in leadership. There are many more, and they all can be taught.

How do you teach leadership? You could take a class, buy several opinionated books by authors who've 'been there', or participate in leadership seminars, workshops, or programs sponsored by your company--if they are available. These cost too much and in the end the principles of leadership are the same ones taught decades ago. This book is all you need to learn the key principles of leadership and for pennies on the dollar compared to what's out there. In this book you'll learn the theories and principles of motivation, decision making, influencing others, leading a team, and building your network for success. Now it's time to relax and open up to our first chapter. Let's go.

TABLE OF CONTENTS

1. Motivation

2. Individual Decision Making

3. Group Decision Making

4. Leading Teams

5. How To Influence Others

6. Building Your Network

7. Conclusion

8. Appendix: Psychoanalytical Surveys

MOTIVATION

Leadership guru Warren Bennis wrote a 1989 book *On Becoming a Leader* and a 1993 book *An Invented Life: Reflections on Leadership and Change,* that are required reading for many leadership development programs. In these books he aims to make a distinction between a **manager** or the archetypical 'boss' as we've seen in movies such as the Office Space and a **leader** that inspires, motivates, and leads by example. A few examples of this distinction are as follows:

- The manager administers; the leader innovates.
- The manager maintains; the leader develops.
- The manager focuses on systems and structure; the leader focuses on people.
- The manager relies on control; the leader inspires trust.

- The manager accepts reality; the leader investigates it.
- The manager asks how and when; the leader asks what and why.
- The manager does things right; the leader does the right thing.
- The manager has his eye on the bottom line; the leader has his eye on the horizon.

This is not to say that one must be one or the other. Managers are needed to run the day to day operations. They are vital to the success of a company. However, for a company to succeed it cannot just tackle known problems, it has to be able to adapt to the changing environment, and this ability to inspire and lead change from the top to bottom of an organizational chart is what leadership is all about. An organization can have an individual who is both a leader and a manager or they can separate the roles. Steve Jobs was a classic example of both a manager and a leader in his early career, but managing people is an art form and he slowly transitioned exclusively to the position of leader on his return to Apple.

Motivation is at the heart of leadership. Understanding how to motivate one's employees can be a key strategy in improving sales and improving the product or service. The typical notion is that everyone is motivated by money and having a robust commission program will drive sales. Although true in some industries especially when the product is hated by the salespeople, it is *not always* true. There are many companies that switched to a flat salary for their salespeople and have not seen a dip in sales. In fact, sales improved. This is further illustrated in Daniel Pink's book *Drive*. The main takeaway is that motivation is linked to autonomy, mastery, and purpose once a person's basic needs are already satisfied. That's why commission still works but again-- it's more common in companies where the sales people hate their job or the product, or people's basic needs have not been met which makes monetary incentives powerful enough to get them to sell sell sell. A summary of some of the insights from Daniel Pink's book *Drive* can be viewed here <https://youtu.be/u6XAPnuFjJc>. Next, we will learn about content theories (Maslow; Intrinsic & Extrinsic) and process theories (expectancy; equity) of motivation. Understanding these will help you understand employees and co-workers better.

ABRAHAM MASLOW HIERARCHY OF NEEDS

Maslow, A. Motivation and Personality (2nd ed.) Harper & Row, 1970.

SELF-ACTUALIZATION
Pursue Inner Talent
Creativity Fulfillment

SELF-ESTEEM
Achievement Mastery
Recognition Respect

BELONGING - LOVE
Friends Family Spouse Lover

SAFETY
Security Stability Freedom from Fear

PHYSIOLOGICAL
Food Water Shelter Warmth

Maslow's Hierarchy: this is a pyramid of basic needs where people can't focus on the next need up the pyramid without first achieving the need below it. It begins with the Physiological such food and shelter, moves up to Safety, then Belonging, followed by Self-Esteem, and finally Self-Actualization. While we've achieved the first two steps of the pyramid in developed countries, the last three are difficult to achieve for most people.

Alderfer's ERG Theroy

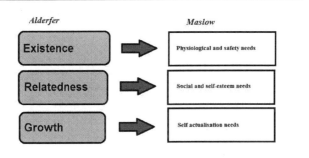

Clayton Alderfer took Maslow's needs and grouped them into a model he calls **ERG** for Existence, Relatedness, and Growth. The difference is that he didn't see one need depending on the other but rather that all needs are happening at the same. If for example an employee doesn't have enough growth opportunities in a company, then they will focus their energy on fulfilling the relatedness need by socializing with coworkers. This allows us to approach people in general through five lens instead of trying to figure out where on the pyramid they're currently fixed.

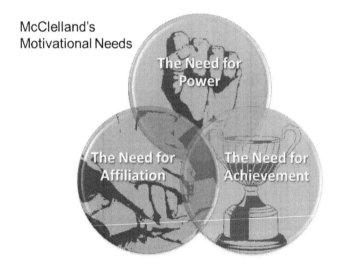

McClelland's
Motivational Needs

The Need for Power

The Need for Affiliation

The Need for Achievement

David McClelland in his 1961 book *The Achieving Society* described three motivational forces that are inherent in all of us (technically in 86% of us according to research) but that depending on our life experience one of these is a dominant force. Thus making it important for hiring managers to know which is the dominant force in their applicants as it fits the job description. The need for power, affiliation, and achievement are known as the **Three Needs Theory** in the context of managing employees. In his subsequent article, published in the 1977 Harvard Business Review article *Power is the Great Motivator*, McClelland found that those with a high need for power and low need for affiliation were more likely in top management. Those with a high need for achievement usually don't make it to top management as they value being challenged which often is not the case and their performance and attitude reflect that. Lastly, those with a high need for affiliation are not good managers but they are very happy workers.

Reward Theory for Motivation:

When it comes to rewarding your employees

to drive motivation, so called **extrinsic motivation**, there are two common theories to know. Expectancy and Equity.

Expectancy Theory: This was developed by Victor Vroom of the Yale School of Management in 1964. It consists of three types of extrinsic motivators, namely, that effort will lead to performance (expectancy), that performance will lead to an outcome (instrumentality) and that the outcome is a reward that is desired (valence). Valence refers to the value a person places on a reward whether positive, negative, or neutral. The first comes into play in designing a training program or new protocol, the second in the day to day operations, and the third is the most important in that if the reward is not something that is *desired* then there will neither be effort nor performance. The key to using expectancy theory is to first find out what your employees desire, and then assign them tasks with a clear outcome to look forward to and milestones along the way that show that their effort has paid off. Celebrate those milestones as it validates their expectancy that their efforts lead to performance, and reward them with what they desire.

Equity Theory: developed in 1969 by J. Stacy Adams, a behavioral psychologist. it implies that employees are motivated to balance the inputs with the outputs of their work environment. This is very subjective which is why a leader needs to have their finger on the pulse on their employee morale. If one employee feels they are underpaid then they will underperform. If an employee has been offered more than they feel they deserve then they will try to work harder. It is this need to create balance that can be a strong motivator. Think of the startup companies that offer unlimited vacations. It's been shown that the employees in these companies actually take fewer vacations than typically expected.

INDIVIDUAL DECISION MAKING

Simon Herbert, a prolific scholar with more than 1000 publications, came up with a definition for rational decision making in 1947 that consisted of intelligence gathering, design, and choice. He pragmatically hypothesized that no amount of intelligence gathering would reveal all information, thus prompting him to come up with the **theory of bounded rationality**, or in other words, our rationality is bounded by the information we have. On the other end of the spectrum, when we are flooded with information, we do not have the time to process it all or remember it all and just like when we have little information, we end up using **heuristics**, or shortcuts to this information in order to make judgments. A leader should be aware of the biases involved with our natural inclination to create shortcuts to information. At its simplest manifestation, an employee who feels overwhelmed with information will take shortcuts and make assumptions, similar to an employee with too little information.

Let's look at a few additional examples encountered often by business leaders:

Anchoring: It is a very common tactic used in negotiation where the first offer anchors the negotiation to some set level and from there adjustments are made. Similarly, we tend to anchor on one number, fact, or concept in a sea of information or infer a fact from little information. We then make adjustments to this anchor based on new information, but we've already convinced ourselves that the truth must be close to this anchor. Business managers are often known to anchor their opinion of employees on a strength or a weakness and then make small adjustments over time. That's why first impressions are important whether you are entry level or moving up the corporate ladder.

To learn about **anchoring** in the context of

negotiation, be sure to pick up a copy of the Concise Reads *The Art of Negotiation*, one of our best sellers.

Naive Diversification: When a leader faces multiple choices at the same time but they have limited information or don't understand the information completely, they tend to pick choices that are consistent with multiple strategies rather than a unified strategy. If you reach this point, it means you need more information to make a better decision. There is no reason to execute multiple strategies and hope that one hits the mark.

Sunk Cost Fallacy: also known as **Escalation of Commitment**, is the phenomenon that the most common reason why a choice was made is because it was made previously. Managers who invest in a project will continue to invest despite increasing costs and decreasing revenues. The psychological threshold required for them to choose a different strategy has increased by virtue of investing (psychologically) in the first choice. Also known as **Gambler's fallacy**.

Use these concept when evaluating both your own individual decision making as well as that of your employees.

GROUP DECISION MAKING

"The understanding that underlies the right decision grows out of the clash and conflict of divergent opinions and out of the serious consideration of competing alternatives."

Peter Drucker

Nominal group theory/technique (NGT): NOT a decision making tool. It is used to generate as many possible **creative options** by harnessing the power of group dynamics. This technique was developed by Andre Delbecq and Andrew H. Van de Ven. It starts by gathering your team and then involves problem identification, solution generation, and decision making. You might think this is similar to brainstorming and then taking a group vote. The actual difference lies in the method of tallying the votes. Each member of the group gives their own solutions to the problem, then as a group, the solutions are ranked from best to worst. The important lesson from NGT that has been borrowed by think tanks and other groups like the product design company IDEO is that of divergence before convergence. In other words, you want to generate as many solutions as possible hence **prompting every member** of the group and then allowing for some discussion to possibly mix and match solutions. Once all that could be said has been said, then convergence occurs and a solution is selected.

Research into the use of NGT has shown that requiring individuals to write down their ideas independently prior to group discussion generates more solutions. The fact that every member participated has also been shown to provide greater individual satisfaction and sense of accomplishment from the group meeting.

Value-Driven-Design (VDD): VDD is a design process that allows for multiple disciplines to come together for a solution to complex multi-disciplinary problems or products. It was coined by James Sturges at Lockheed Martin in 2006. It then was used by the American Institute of Aeronautics and Astronautics. It is often interchangeable with the US Defense Advanced Research Projects Agency model of **Value-Centric-Design**. In the digital world, a similar model is known as **Agile software development**. All three focus on prioritizing work on the most valuable aspect of a design instead of being bogged down with performance metrics. It helps to simplify the design and focus attention on the most important tasks. First, a value model is created which is an objective function that ranks the items that would bring the most value (economic value) to the final product. This is an objective value model. The design process then begins with several alternatives, whereby one attribute is sacrificed for additional resources in another, and a total score is calculated based on the ranking of the value model. This is slightly different from a very similar group framework known as **Multi**

Attribute Utility or MAU model that builds a subjective **utility** model based on the utility to different stakeholders.

Multi-Attribute Utility model (MAU): The MAU model asks us to build the utility model based on agreed upon criteria. The next step is then to offer alternative solutions. We repeat this process when we factor in future scenarios where the criteria might change. In both contexts, we test our alternative solutions against the criteria.

The frameworks for group decision making are pretty robust and templates are available for free online. Whether to use VDD or MAU depends on what your objective is whether it is to **maximize economic value** (and hence profit) or to **maximize utility** of the stakeholders involved (whether partners or clients). The frameworks focus you to design with a purpose and not to just design the best product out there. Similar to our Nominal group theory, this requires input from everyone at the table.

Lastly, as an aside, there is common term in the industry for outsourcing the design process but wanting control of the criteria used, whether it is a value model or utility model. These criteria or specifications are typically seen when government contracts with product or service design firms. This is known as **Value Based Acquisition** or VBA. This is more suitable if your organization does not have the necessary expertise to problem solve the solutions but have a strong understanding of the required criteria.

These are some of the basic methods of group decision making, with the NGT being the most prevalent in higher level management meetings. In fact, John F. Kennedy used that very technique when he assembled a team of experts to deal with the Cuban missile crisis.

HOW TO INFLUENCE OTHERS

To build a high performing team it is important to set aside personal agendas as they can derail team objectives. Engaging in politics is differentiated from a team member being savvy in that the former is for personal gain, while the latter is leveraging people of influence to meet a team's agenda. Thus, it is important to realize which team member is engaging in politics and which is being savvy for the team's benefit.

Do not engage with other team members in political ambitions as it is often quite obvious to the team and will ultimately hurt team morale. Focus on the objective when building a team. This involves:

1) Setting the objective of the team

2) Providing the team with all the resources

they need (don't ask them to go looking for resources)

3) Allocate the work fairly

4) Break up the objective into milestones so that the team can see progress and feel motivated, and lastly

5) Build tasks with <u>increasing responsibility</u> so that team members see a <u>growth</u> in their role as progress is made. This last one is critical, because if a team member feels they are doing the same job--one job--for the duration of a team project, their motivation will wane and their productivity will drop.

The Art of Persuasion: It often seems like a natural born gift for some people to be able to persuade others. It's not. There are a set of basic principles that you can follow. These principles are derived from Robert Cialdini's article in the Harvard Business Review on *Harnessing the Science of Persuasion.* The principles are as follows:

1) **Liking**: by genuinely liking others they like you in return. By praising others, they like you in return. By liking you, it becomes much easier to persuade. In fact, studies have shown that consumers tend to purchase more items from a salesperson they like than one they haven't established that rapport with.

2) **Reciprocity**: this is as simple as giving before receiving. Employees who receive benefits from employers tend to feel a sense of obligation to give back when asked to stay with the company longer or to help out with a project. Similarly, if a co-worker goes out of their way to help another co-worker, they are more likely than not to persuade them to help in a later

instance. Just make sure not to ask for help too soon after you volunteer your aid, or you risk seeming transactional.

3) **Social Proof**: people are more likely to be persuaded if someone else with similar interests has already been persuaded. Thus, if pitching a new initiative to employees, it is in your best interest to have a veteran employee endorse it. The same is true in politics and the importance of endorsements.

4) **Consistency**: People who make small public commitments to something they value are more likely to make larger commitments just to stay consistent with their belief system. For a leader, if you want the employees to adopt a large change, first get them to openly (in public or by putting it in writing such as a signature on a memo or petition) accept a small change, and then ask them later to accept the larger change. The important caveat here is

that the small change has to align with their belief system. So if you want a tardy employee to be on time, then ask him or her to talk to another employee who has been tardy about the value of a good work ethic.

5) **Authority**: People are more likely to be persuaded by an expert or authority on a subject matter rather than by the authority implicit in being someone's boss. Thus, it behooves leaders to showcase their expertise in a subject matter prior to asking others to follow their lead. Be mindful of how you showcase your background, use examples, or answer difficult questions, and don't just state that you are an authority figure. This is an extremely effective technique during company presentations.

6) **Scarcity**: People want what is scarce more than gaining what is abundant. This has been shown in multiple

experiments. The key for the leader is in framing offers in the form of how <u>exclusive</u> or <u>limited</u> they are. A simple example is when choosing an employee to complete a task, make sure to let them know that you specifically picked them for the job because they are one of only a handful of people who can get the job done. Sounds silly, but it works.

Dale Carnegie's Principles on How to Influence Others: what is interesting is that the science of persuasion is not new. In fact, you will see many similarities from Dale Carnegie's principles published in 1936. The principles for making others like you can be boiled down to showing genuine interest and liking them from the onset. I highly recommend that book, if only to see how much thought was put in to learning the art of persuasion. More specifically and for your enjoyment the principles are as follows:

1. Don't criticize, condemn or complain.

2. Give honest, sincere appreciation.

3. Arouse in the other person an eager want.

4. Become genuinely interested in other people.

[Carnegie emphasized being genuine multiple times because it affects your body language so much and it takes away any feeling of being false or fake in your enthusiasm.]

5. Smile.

6. Remember that a person's name is to that person the most important sound in any language.

7. Be a good listener. Encourage others to talk about themselves.

8. Talk in terms of the other person's interest.

9. Make the other person feel important - and do so sincerely.

10 The only way to get the best of an argument is to avoid it.

Relationship building is foundational to Influencing others. Learning how to build relationships should be a focus of your career. We will emphasize this again in the last section, *Building Your Network*, because if you remember one thing from this book, it is that relationships determine how effective you are as a leader. A study that looked at the emotional intelligence of managers and leaders found that leaders more so than managers had significantly higher emotional intelligence scores. Enough said.

LEADING TEAMS

When teams form in an organization, it is not to exchange or share information. With the advent of technology and communications, Information can be shared in a number of different way outside the setting of a group meeting. When teams meet, it is during a decision point in the process workflow. Efficient organizations and leaders know how to value the strengths of individuals and utilize the team setting for tasks that are better handled as a group rather than to disseminate individual assignments. Let's explore this topic some more.

Deciding on the structure of Teams: The makeup of the team varies, and so should your leadership style. This is a very broad topic because of the diversity of teams and leadership styles to deal with these teams as well as the diversity of projects and cultures across organizations. However, we should at least learn some basics. The most common types of team formations are:

1. **Problem-Solving Teams**: This is the typical small group structure across departments meeting with senior leadership or employees within the same department meeting with middle management. These teams meet regularly and discuss active problems, offer solutions, and give updates on past problems that are being actively resolved. There is a cadence to these meetings so as to structure a specific time to bring up problems to leadership.

2. **Independent Teams**: These are teams that don't need to report to senior leadership, and tackle problems directly as they arise. They are given authority and autonomy to solve problems as they see fit. The members of those teams are carefully chosen because

they are motivated, driven, and have bought into the culture of the organization. You can spot them easily because they always refer to the company as 'our company' and the customers as 'our customers'.

3. **Cross-Functional Teams**: These are teams made up of experts from different business units in the department or company. They are usually brought together to work on a new project that requires everyone's input and buy-in. These teams can be difficult to manage because they are made up of educated, driven, ambitious individuals who consider themselves leaders in their respective fields. That's why they require <u>effective leadership</u>, and we will stress this when we talk next about the concept of interdependence.

Leading Type-A Highly Educated Individuals: This comes as no surprise that leading other 'leaders' is a challenge. Type A personalities are driven by complexity, challenge, and professional stimulation. They do not like to be led, and owing to the greater degree of expertise, the disadvantage is that they often reach conflict when trying to work together. The advantage of leading such an independent team is that the leader does not have to be the domain expert. In fact, the team prides itself in its own expertise. A cornerstone to one's interaction with such a team is making it clear that there is *interdependence*. This means that the clever team member's expertise will complement or supplement another member's expertise or even the leader's expertise. Establishing this interdependence early on has enabled better collaboration in a Harvard Business Review study of organizational leadership. After establishing that the team is interdependent, the leader's focus should shift from managing the discussion to one facilitating discussion. One approach is to use the nominal group theory of decision making with modifications when assigning tasks. This means asking for the input of the 'experts', taking their point of view into consideration, and asking them how soon they can deliver. As a leader of such a team, you will notice that they will relish the idea of finishing the deliverable before the deadline and will be even more excited if it was their solution that was chosen. Another important principle in this context is to demonstrate what's known as 'executive presence'. This means taking a step back from managing the details and projecting confidence that the team can handle the deliverable. Establishing interdependence, taking the role of facilitator, asking for their expert input, and demonstrating executive presence while remaining hands off will allow you to form a highly productive and efficient team.

4. **Remote Teams:** In some organizations, the company talent is geographically separated. In such cases, the act of collaboration can be frustrating if the wrong technology is

used. The members of such a team also lack competitive motivation because of minimal face to face interaction and do not initiate as much collaboration online as they would have if they were closer to each other. This is not to say that remote teams cannot work. They can. The challenges of this new work environment prompted a new research discipline called **computer supported cooperative work** or **network** and we will discuss that next.

Computer Supported Cooperative Network/Work (CSCN/CSCW): This was first coined by Irene Greif and Paul M. Cashman in 1984 to describe enabling technology to support collaboration in the workplace. CSCN is an academic research field focused on studying how groups work together and finding the technology that will improve their productivity. The CSCN field has identified multiple criteria for effective group work including *Awareness* of each other's activities, *Articulation work* where work can be divided into parts and then grouped in the next meeting, and *Appropriation* where a team can tailor a given technology to suit their collaborative needs.

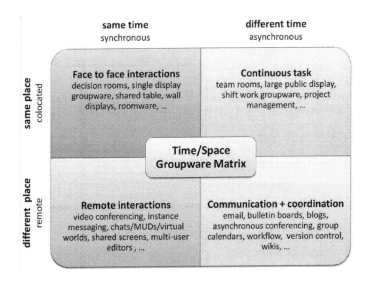

The CSCW matrix is divided into two axes, one that defines groups based on proximity and the other based on whether the work needs to be synchronous or can be asynchronous. The cells then define the best possible options for the four different scenarios. For example for work that is remote and asynchronous, to improve productivity and meet the criteria of CSCN previously mentioned such as Awareness, a group calendar as well as wikis, blogs, or bulletin boards need to be established. For work that is remote but synchronous team requires video conferencing, instant messaging, shared screens, and cloud-based versioning technology for multiple editors (such as google drive).

5. **Organizational Leadership:** This was how teams were formed a few decades ago. They were based on formal hierarchies and involved receiving routine predictable tasks from the boss. Idea generation, discussion, and decision making was reserved for the senior leadership only. While this works for routine tasks, it is less productive for new projects or tasks that require creativity or a change in operations. Additionally productivity has been show to correlate with buy-in from employees or what the literature refers to as **Theory Y**.

To paraphrase. **Theory X** is where expectations are set and performance is measured against those expectations, and **Theory Y**, is where a leader's job <u>moved from setting expectations</u> to providing all the necessary resources for their employees to do their best work. Theory Y is linked with the millennial generation that requires things like autonomy and a nurturing environment with a flat hierarchy to produce results. This goes back to our earlier emphasis on relationship building and emotional intelligence where leaders understand what motivates their employees and find that which inspires them to perform better.. Empirical research into the relationship between emotional intelligence and executive leadership was limited up until recently when researchers found that leaders with higher emotional intelligence were more likely to lead using transformative rather than transactional leadership.

6. **Matrix Structure**: Initially seen in consulting firms, it is now a very common team structure. Employees in the matrix have more than one boss. They have the department manager who tasks them with the day to day duties and a project or program manager who was tasked with assembling his or her own team to complete a new project. This structure was created more so to separate the functional manager from the team leader so as to maximize their effectiveness with the employees. When recruiters advertise that they need someone comfortable with a matrix organization, they are explicitly asking for applications from individuals who feel comfortable wearing many different hats and reporting to different 'bosses'. This is a higher stress team organization, but for industries like consulting, it is important for efficiency to pull people from one project to another as needed.

BUILDING YOUR NETWORK

A leader's social network is an integral part of success. Organizational leaders are distinct compared to their counterpart managers in their ability to use their network to get things done. Networks are developed to improve operations, to accommodate the leader's career trajectory, or to support the business goals. What you'll find in the literature is by far, developing leaders fret over building social networks but those who overcome it are better for it. This inflection point of overcoming whatever personal reservations one has in building a robust network is pivotal in one's career. I want to stress that you should think of your social capital in the following three types of networking: operational, personal, and strategic. Let's look at how they differ.

Operational Networking: This comes most naturally by virtue of the work environment.

Leaders have to work with their peers, their superiors, and a whole set of organizational characters. The operational network will help you produce results and then push you to the next stage of your career. The problem is that the old network is of no use to you in your new position. Now what? That's why it is important to keep an open mind and build relationships with people who may not necessarily work with you today, but may work with you in the future, or whom you can leverage to build stronger relationships with different divisions. Build relationships across the aisle, don't stay in your own division.

Personal Networking: This one is the hardest for aspiring leaders. Many ask why spend additional time out of work to build relationships. The answer is simple: because people are what make or break your career. There are many get togethers from alumni events, company sponsored events, charities, volunteer groups, etc. Even if you do begin to spend part of your week building personal relationships, the question that comes up is whether you should talk to as many people as possible? Maybe you should see who is attending an event, then research their backgrounds so you have some talking points? No. This is not an operative mission and you are not undercover. The strongest relationships are those borne of similar interest. Additionally, conversation flows when you talk about something that interests you. You are not trying to using broad brush strokes. This network is meant to be **stronger** than your operational network. So much so, that if you're in a jam, or need mentoring, or need a referral or introduction, this is the network you would go to first.

Strategic Networking: This last network can take up the most time but also yield the most benefit. Strategic networking means actively picking the people whose support you want or who are key to moving you further in your career. Because this is not based on working together like operational networking, or based on mutual interests like personal networking, the strategic network requires much more leg work, one on one conversations, and even lending support to one of their causes so that they could lend support to yours down the line. As a leader moves up the ladder, they will find that they spend less time with operational networking and more time with strategic networking to build stakeholder support. Leaders at the very top spend a significant amount of time on speeches, meetings, discussions, etc.. to build support for themselves, for their ideas, and for their goals. Hopefully that answers the age old questions of when do senior leaders actually work? Strategic networking is their work. Start by thinking what your goals are, where you want to be, and whose support you want, then begin forcing these relationships slowly over months (and years sometimes) so as not to actually seem forced.

CONCLUSION

Hopefully you were able to glean the major principles of leadership in under a day. You'll see many frameworks, tools, and buzzwords used to explain the challenges of leadership. Just remember that leadership is a job about people. It's not about coming in early and staying late, although that type of servant leadership wins you points on the credibility scale. It's not about dressing sharp and holding your back straight, although those can help with persuasion. Leadership is about relationship building. Can you build a relationship with anyone? If you can, then everything else in this book becomes a breeze. If you can't, then you've just been given a set of tools from motivating, to influencing, to mastering group dynamics. I hope it serves you well in your future career and I wish you the best of luck. For additional titles in the concise reads business success series, be sure to check under my name or under concise reads in your physical or online bookstore. If this was helpful, please also leave a positive review which as we learned with expectancy theory, it will reinforce my effort, and I will be motivated to write more titles.

APPENDIX: PSYCHOANALYTICAL SURVEYS

These are psychoanalytical surveys that will help you learn more about yourself as a manager and leader. They are provided here for future personal discovery if you are so inclined. If the links are broken, a simple google search will take you there as they are all free except for the Myers Briggs test which requires a small fee.

- Tolerance for Ambiguity (TFA) Survey: <http://www4.ncsu.edu/unity/users/p/padilla/www/435-Leadership/Scale-%20tolerance%20of%20ambiguity.pdf >
- Psychodynamic Approach: Survey<http://people.uncw.edu/nottinghamj/documents/slides6/Northouse 6e%20Ch13%20PsychodynamicMyers-Briggs%20Survey.pdf>

- Skills Inventory: <https://www.mindtools.com/pages/article/get-started.htm>
- Style Questionnaire <http://duluth.umn.edu/careers/inventories/personality_test_intro.html>
- Leadership Trait Questionnaire: <http://www.dr-hatfield.com/leadership/pdf/Leadership%20Traits%20Questionnaire.pdf>
- Myers Briggs Type indicator: <http://www.myersbriggs.org/my-mbti-personality-type/mbti-basics/>

Made in the USA
Lexington, KY
19 December 2017